AF439398

reciprocal relationship between predator and prey. She explores scientific facts amid beautiful images in "Coyote Singing": "…poignant enough to perfume the dark." Her blossoms unlock to songs "known only to the feral-winged and wild of heart." From observation of lichens as "mesmerizing fractals that underscore this world's reflective nature" to honey badger who declares in first person, "I eat and eat, return from the dead again and again," Irving weaves surprise, candor and delight within ultimate theme and meaning about the reciprocal dynamic interaction between predators and prey. She navigates the natural world with elegant simplicity and sophisticated, fact-based complexity—couching all of it within musical language and unforgettable metaphors that might (if we read closely enough) help us all know predator and prey as ourselves, but perhaps with a more understanding and compassionate view.

~ Charlotte Renk has twice won Poetry Society of Texas Catherine Case Lubbe Manuscript Prize: in 2017 for *This Great Turtle Heart: The Tao of Turtlism*; and in 2009, for *These Holy Hungers: Secret Yearnings from an Empty Cup*. Her work has also appeared in numerous publications including Kalliope, Mochila Review, New Texas '95, and others; and in the anthologies *Her Texas; A Texas Garden of Verses*; and *Writing Texas*. Dr. Renk recently retired after teaching many years at Trinity Valley College

Predator/Prey

Predator/Prey

Christine Irving

Aurochs Press
Denton, TX

Christine Irving /Aurochs Press

Predator/Prey   Christine Irving. -- 1st ed.
ISBN 9798418513403

Dedicated

to all the many incredible women and men
who spend their lives in the field
tormented by flies, scratched by thorns,
sucked upon by leeches, burnt by the sun
and battered by gales, to study
our fellow creatures
in their own habitats. Your patience
has added immeasurably
to our understanding
of the world and ourselves.
I cannot thank you enough.

Acknowledgements

Thanks to Beth Honeycutt, Bob Schinzel and Michal Minassian for critiquing so many of these poems with care and attention. Your perception and intelligence never fails to enhance and clarify.

And to the Poetry Society of Texas, which continues to provide a forum for poets of every ilk to showcase and refine their work: Thank you for making the camaraderie of others dedicated to crafting perception and vision available to all of us poets. I am grateful be chosen as this year's recipient of the Catherine Lubbe Manuscript Award.

As always, I owe undying gratitude to my beloved husband John Irving: proofreader, editor and faithful fan whose interest in and attention to my work provides unfaltering encouragement and support.

Contents

Christine Irving

Introduction

I learned about totem animals in a workshop that began with three brief statements: Animals manifest on the spiritual plane as well as in the material. Through lucid dreaming, ritual or trance a person may connect and come into relationship with the spirit of a particular animal. The attraction between human and totem is based on an affinity between a person's own nature and the characteristics of a particular animal.

Next, the facilitator showed us a bag of clay, told us to take what we wanted, find a quiet, secluded place in the woods and begin playing with the raw clay until an animal emerged. Eventually, I returned with a rabbit. It was very disappointing. I would have preferred a larger fiercer animal– a predator in fact, as opposed to one I considered weak, meek and uninteresting.

But rabbit it was, at least for the rest of the afternoon, which consisted of various interactions with our newly discovered animal spirits. The final instruction we received was to gather round the firepit and take turns dancing our animal! At first, hopping around the fire felt awkward and ridiculous, but slowly I began to feel more rabbity. Crouching and leaping went from arduous to easy as playacting became play. I found that I could hunker down in stillness and rest between leaps. By the time my turn ended, my identification with rabbit had increased tenfold. I took my little clay image home and decided to give rabbit a chance.

Over time, I began to understand why we were encouraged to study and understand the behavior of the real creature– the behavior of an animal can offer both a mirror and metaphor for one's own actions and predilections.

Animals can be either predator or prey and many are both. Either way, the relationship is lifelong, warrants exploration and adds to the potential for greater self-knowledge. In studying predator and prey one encounters the incontrovertible evidence that within our biosphere life and death, rather than being opposite entities, comprise an organic whole.

It's also beneficial to consider the symbolic import of totem animals. Symbols survive in the collective unconscious for a reason. Their meanings reflect the embedded wisdom of ancestors who lived intimately with the natural world for thousands of years before modernity cursed us with a false belief in human difference and superiority.

Rabbit has become an important part of my voyage of self-discovery. She's taught me to face my fears, understand how I freeze or bolt in the face of confrontation. I've learned that generosity is a part of my nature, but needs discernment, which is where one of rabbit's predators, great horned owl, comes in. An owl's far-seeing eye can perceive the consequence of each action much more clearly than earthbound rabbit.

Two of my early poems about rabbit and great horned owl mix symbolism and physical reality. It's a combination I've continued to use throughout my work. The slightly surreal atmosphere this mix produces represents the ways in which the natural physical world interacts with the more elusive realm of spirit. Those two poems appeared in my first book, *Be a Teller of Tales*, but they were the seeds for this current endeavor, which has taught me so much about the habits and habitats of the animal pairs I've chosen to include.

Predator/Prey is only the tip of an iceberg of facts, figures, stories, and studies. I spent many more hours researching than writing. The most arresting fact for me is that predator and prey drive each other to become more – swifter, smarter, wiser, more agile and adept. A mutation in one triggers a mutation in another.

Science is just beginning to understand what an enormous factor mutuality plays in the workings of our planet. Again and again, as I researched these animals' precious lives, co-dependence emerged as the most important factor in their survival and success as a species.

I could not complete this tiny bestiary without including us two-leggeds, who like to forget we belong squarely within these ranks. Hence, the final poems in this collection which touch on the human condition.

One thing I know is true– everything is connected. As physicist Christopher Toth once said, "Everything causes a scintillation."

Christine Irving, November 2021

Change or Die

It's not about the chase,
the catcher or the caught,
red teeth and claws,
or Bambi's mother
lying dead on the side of the road.

Change is nature's only game,
played for life's highest stakes—
mutuality its joker, the card
that gets us out of jail.

We exist in a net of connections
so sensitive the merest flutter of wing,
the faintest footfall, touches all—
each vibration instigating reaction,
each reaction soliciting response.

Some ancient success stories
need only minute adjustments
to their blueprints, small internal
mutations, modifications
gone unrecorded in fossil records.

Evolution picks up its pace
in families like our own; only
mutuality cuts across the board
leveling the playing field, conserving
resources, enhancing survival.

Christine Irving

Even the shark has its remora,
the crocodile its plover bird,
the ant its aphid, while root tip
to root tip diverse species of tree
inform, feed and advise each other.

Yet homo sapiens, purported
to be wise, can't seem to learn,
refuse to remember
the need to co-exist.

A Paean for All Pollinators

All praises to the pollinators,
beloved bees, hummingbirds, bats,
beetles, wasps, ants, thrip and midge.

We thank you for food and flowers,
apples, almonds, alfalfa, blueberries,
strawberries, cucumbers, squash, melons.

You nourish our bodies,
feed our hearts with beauty.

For you we will plant lemon balm,
lavender and thyme, allow milkweed,
wild daisies, asters and goldenrod
purchase on our properties.

If only you will stay, blackberries
may loop around our fence posts,
fallen branches lie ungathered
in the corners of our yards.

Dear white-winged dove,
dear lesser long-nosed bat,
we cannot live without you.
Your fate, our own. Our destiny
inextricably entwined with yours.

Christine Irving

The Lesser Long-Nosed Bat

Each wing is a muscle, stretched to translucence,
strong enough to carry her home to give birth
in the cave of her ancestors. By day, she roosts
among her kind, inside stone fissures, old mine
shafts, ancient wormholes bored by gouts of lava
through cooling molten rock.

At dusk, black-on-black whirlpools
of wings explode in spiraling clouds,
eddying above dark fields of flowers.
Each plant, blossoming once each lifetime,
opens to the darkling hours when bats
fly to feed and pollinate.

A nectar trail of night-blooming blue agave
leads north through perfumed midnights
from southern Mexico to Arizona. Without
the lesser long-nosed bat, agave and saguaro
fade away. Bees, moths, lizards, hummingbirds,
finches, and field mice desert the desert.

If tequila disappears, man's desire for drink
may save our tiny keystone mutualist. So many
livelihoods and creatures rest upon her wings,
each wing a muscle stretched translucent thin,
strong enough to carry her home to give birth.

Of Moths and Their Ear Mites

Moths fly their night ways silently,
fat wings furred to muffle flight.
Sharp ears alert to shrilling squeaks,
evade the whistling swoop of bats.

Baby mites begin their lives
born on moth's shoulder,
curled tight inside
infinitesimal shells.

They hatch into hunger,
directed by dreams to mewl
through buff-brown thickets
seeking the moth's ear.

Nibbling tender whorls and ridges,
scuttle tiny feet across the tympani,
tapping out irritating rhythms
until their host goes deaf.

Could be a classic tragedy–
the mite, unable to control greed,
disarms the moth till both fall prey,
lost to bat's dark belly.

life's a better playwright
than Shakespeare dared to be.
First mite to leave the nest sets a course
for all the rest, exuding sticky substance

he lays a trail so tantalizing
siblings follow single file, dripping
the same sweet syrup, never deviating,
eating each other's footprints as they go.

One auricle alone goes deaf.
The cock-eared moth
flies on to meet and mate.

Canis Vulgaris

*The cosmos is interesting rather than perfect
and everything is not part of some greater
plan or is all necessarily under control.*
~Starhawk, *The Spiral Dance*

Coyote pooped last night, upon
a high point of crystalline pink rock.
Wind, frost, sun and rain
had burnished the surface black,
disguising luminescence
until stone striking stone chipped
the dark patina exposing its rosy heart.

Lichens grow here,
pale green amoeba-shaped splotches,
mesmerizing fractals that underscore
this world's reflective nature, wherein
earthen elements reshape themselves
in ceaseless imitation of each other.

Inside this miniature terrain, outcrop
becomes mountain range—
a stand of cactus, forest.
Needle-sharp spines shoot shadows
straight as sentinels, marking hours
like tiny sundials keeping cosmic time.

Christine Irving

Coyote's scat contains a scatter of small pits.
He feasts on berry bushes near the creek,
travels happily between worlds, finding
no ambiguity in navigating landscapes
macro, micro, rustic or urbane.
His trickster nature, mutable
as a chameleon's skin, bestows
a certain savoir faire, lets him
fit in anywhere, disdaining
domestication, flaunting freedom
from any old peak.

Coyote Singing

I am Song Dog
Bringer of Light,
Keeper of the Dark.

I scout the perimeters
of blind spots, mapping
your shadow. Scratching,
farting, spitting, I test
your boundaries, seeking
the perspective of high places.
I know your secrets
because they are mine.

Hilltops, ridgelines, granite
outcroppings tumbled into boulders,
are where I drop my scat—
more signpost than graffiti—
scribbled across fixed points
of destination and territory.

Mostly I drift,
ignoring borders
wander east, south,
west and north,
coast to coast,
making each inch mine,
creating my own myth,
singing songs of freedom,
loneliness, loss
and unadulterated joy.

Christine Irving

Detail

Kurt Vonnegut imagined God
as an artistic director, creating
one universe after another,
leaving behind each finished opus,
to move toward other cosmic canvases.

If so, perhaps Her aura lingers.
Desire to create still potent enough
to manifest intentions, make dreams
come true, corroborate prayer's power.

They say, *God is in the details*.

Coyote pups are born with claws
like fine-honed scimitars,
tiny talons sharp enough to shred
a birth canal, rip a female belly
while scrambling for a teat.

But behold!

Miniscule balls of cartilage,
shaped in perfect spheres,
sheathe the twenty razored tips
to shield tender tissue.

Maybe it's just that God loves mothers.

the potency of desire

coyote
       yowls at the moon
   lost in a song
of inchoate longing
     plaintive enough
  to provoke response
        poignant enough
  to perfume the dark

potent as plumeria
jasmine, gardenia

    animal becomes
       moon
cactus
   prairie wind
pulse   current   voice of the void

   … an aching anticipation

no consummation
will ever equal

Christine Irving

The Talisman

My biscuit-colored goddess comes from Oaxaca
smoothed from cool river mud, a traveler like me,
calla lily skirt hiked high, sleeves rolled up
above the elbow, holding a calf beneath each arm,
while two more press against her skirt.

I know she has anticipated me–
stringing cobwebs between lofty ears,
cloaking herself in dust till I find her,
carry her away, carefully wrapped
in the Spanish-infused ink of old newspapers,
out from under the shadow of Monte Albán,
from ruined pyramids and enfeebled gods
hung high above the tree-lined streets
of Santa Maria Atzompa.

Ready to go, whiskers combed neatly back,
breasts pointing firmly forward, eyes wide set
and open, she looks modern as the morning,
but she is older than those ancient ones
whispering above. Born of jungle people
predating priesthood, she flaunts the powers
of vine, blossom, berry, root, stamen and pistil.

Tidy nostrils disclose her animal nature—
small, sturdy muzzle split slightly open
neither smiles nor frowns. She is Creatrix,
Rabbit Mother, mid-wife to poems and pictures,
waving me into the forest, awaiting my return.

the hare

lighter of bone
than rabbit
      hare sleeps
     above ground
   eyes open to the stars
          wild thing
        eschewing domesticity
    relying on stillness
      acceleration
         confusion
waiting till the very(last)moment to
      BOLT
laying labyrinthian trails around its own scent—

shunting
    shifting
  erratically
 back & forth
     sideways   l(eft/righ)t
leading
       coyote dog bobcat
              astray

Christine Irving

When the Wind Picks Up

Pulvis et umbra sumus.
We are but dust and shadow.
~Horace, *The Odes*

Silver dust blurs hare's shadow,
keeping pace like a patient companion soul
as they lope before the nascent storm.
Later, when wind picks up, lifting detritus
of eroded mountain peaks to new heights,
growing in strength and fury, darkening moon,
obliterating shadow, furring dark, obscuring
landmark and scent; we can only hope the jack
attains a burrow, the coyote hunting him
relinquishes chase, unearthing his own shelter
before storm devours the devourer.

Roadkill

Dead owl, ruffled feathers, flattened frog—
tire streaks where pick-up trucks
swerved to hit rabbit, squirrel or armadillo.

Just off the shoulder, a dead doe bloats
half-buried in blue bonnets.
Street diamonds say she didn't go easy.

My fierce rejoicing shames me, reminds me,
I too, once ran a rabbit down.

The children never forgave me, too young
to notice the ditch, the tailgater, the idiot
passing in the face of oncoming traffic.

Etched clearly upon young receptive brains
remains a single strobe-lit shot of frozen bunny,
the unmistakable thump of tires hitting flesh.

Christine Irving

Owls and Their Gods

Owl clacks her bill at dusk.
Chanting? Cursing? Speaking
in owl tongue? Coding memos
Pitching prayers?

Revered, feared, shape-shifting witch
foretelling death or wisdom's messenger
auguring change? Whatever meaning
humankind supposes, these raptors
do not suck the blood of babies, presage
death, or visit doom upon benighted mortals.

The silent-feathered flight of owls
takes place without a thought
for sapient imaginings.

They hoot comments on cloud cover,
contrast the crunchiness of mouse
to mole, broadcast willingness to mate.
No mystic auras trouble their rising moons.

Even if some owl god exists, it's wrought,
like ours, from owl ancestral memory—
T. Rex or Archaeopteryx navigating
Cretaceous canopies, driven by hunger,
thirst, sex or chick to prey.

A Taste for Truffles

I.

Take the false truffle—
rough, round, dung-like and dark
(lacking true truffle flavor) whose fungi
send filaments to twine with chosen
tree root tendrils, suck sugars from sap;
return the favor with minerals and water.
Without false truffles forests fail to thrive.

II.

Take old growth forest—
multi-layered canopies,
convergent limbs and verdant
clumps of dwarf mistletoe, thick
brooms of dead entangled branches,
tall-standing snags, lone ghosts
of trees stripped bare of bark
and weathered white.

III.

Take the northern flying squirrel—
nocturnal in habit, sleeping
by day in reconditioned dens
fashioned by pecking beaks of birds
searching out bugs beneath the bark
of terminal trees. Snags provide perches,
launching pads from which to spread saggy,
baggy flaps of skin, strung loose between
foreleg's wrist and hindleg's ankle
till flaps become wings, flat tails turn rudder.

IV.

Take the Northern Spotted Owl—
yellow beak adept at tearing
preferenced prey– a plump
nocturnal northern flying squirrel,
ace in flight, but less adept aground
digging past leaf litter in search of truffles
whose sturdy spores, resisting digestion,
disperse in pellets spread by squirrels
or scattered wide by predatating owls.

Rat Goddess

Her presence guaranties
all is not lost. Promises
the possibility that what is lost
may be found.

Her sharp eyes discern
the faintest beam of light.
Night is Her playground,
She does not fear the dark.

Her sharp ears discern
the faintest sound,
soft pad of a predator paw.
She knows when to flee,
when to freeze.

Her nose sniffs out
the faintest scent
of wealth or rich corruption.
She follows the money.

She is queen of the zodiac,
running free among the stars,
unbound by gravity or constellations

and oh, how She can swim
dark waters of the mind.

Call on Her to nibble
through knots, unloose
whatever binds.

Christine Irving

She is small, fierce,
chthonic, problematic,
Guardian of the Gem of Thought.

The Rat Queen keeps Her word.
Honored, She becomes an ally.
Denied, She will despoil
every treasured hoard.

Hour of The Rat

> *In ancient China, said to be*
> *the native place of litchi, people*
> *were aware and cautious about*
> *the toxic nature of litchi [seeds].*
> ~NDTV Food, February 4, 2017

New Year's Eve 1924,
my silk-clad crumpled feet slide silently
across the nightingale floor. I know
the trick of never lifting foot from board,
gliding slow and steady, weight balanced
above ankle, like a ballerina dancing en pointe
(As if gangrened toes had ever stood a chance.)

Two years ago, I smashed
the silly music box a suitor presented
three days into this eldest daughter's
first menses; screamed down the house
calling to Jiutian Xuannü the Warrior,
shrieking for her sword. My mother
came instead, more wrathful than any goddess
shut me in a closet with a bucket–
no bread, no water. Three days
with only rats for company,
but they taught me their ways–
surreptitious, clever, calculating, opportunistic.
We bonded. I became an honorary shu.

Christine Irving

They still come when I call, squeaking
in that high-pitched, little-girl voice
men prefer. Last month, I asked them
to bring green lychees, sliced the fruit thin,
dried it on my windowsill, ground it
into powder. Tonight, I'll season
tomorrow's breakfast dumplings,
eaten every New Year's Day for luck.
It's the Year of the Rat. The day of my birth.
I've waited a long time.

Backyard Voyeurs

Four in the morning, night's darkest hour.
Earth turns her gaze from moon's descent
to face dawn's bright arousal
and almost every creature curls in sleep,
paws snugged tight to belly,
head tucked beneath a tail.

Except for rat, whose eyes shine bright
as light bulbs, caught by critter-cam in infra-red.
He scurries here and yon, the skitter of tiny nails
lost beneath the sound of trickling water
feeding our pond, where possum comes
to cadge a drink.

I never thought
I'd come to love a rat-in-residence,
but he displays a lissome grace,
a deft persistent harvesting
I must admire.

Nightly now, we break
every wildlife stricture. Profligate gods
turned unrepentant backyard voyeurs—
we scatter corncobs everywhere
our camera's eye can catch.

Christine Irving

Astarte Dances 'The Dance of Days'

*From Neolithic sites in Anatolia, to
Sumer, Crete, Egypt, Greece and India, cats,
great and small, have been associated with
female figures and divinities.*
~ Alleyn Diesel,
Journal for the Study of Religion

Astarte, veiled in sweet pea, columbine and vetch
walks her golden cats among the yellow hills;
Stars fall to her fingers, clump upon her palm,
deft fingers string a belt with cosmic coin, pluck
the sickle moon, cut long grasses, bind broom,
sweep circles. Her feet stamp out a floor.
Lions settle in place, paws beat time
for jingling hips, dancing belly.

Arms sway, undulating wild hymns
of unrestricted praise to bittersweet
blue Gaia's transient ways, which bind
all beauty, mortal and sublime,
within a noose of ever-ending Time.

Savannah Lullaby

Hey, proud Mama,
babies hiding in the bush—
watch they don't go wandering.

Nose to ground,
you go
slow,
bold,
tail held low.
silhouette flow
kissing sun's gold shadow
across boulder and brush,
dry grass and broken ground,

You spring
without sound,
zebra to ground,
jaws clamping,
      red blood
      pumping.

Small simbas
questing, seeking,
stalking beetles
      need finding,
      need minding,
      need feeding.

Christine Irving

Little paws

pad, pad, pad,
found now,
bellies round now.
Follow close,
no fear.

Mama here,
Mama here.

The Price and Prize of Playing Defense

Flies alight less often
on striped or checkered
patterns. Light and dark
conjunct confuses them.

Zebras, herding
in fly-infested lands,
lift and lower hairs
on black-barred hide
to dissipate heat,
and startle flies away.

Stallions and mares, full grown,
can outrun a big cat. but lions
accelerate faster, spurring
zebra adaptations—
striped skin, longer strides,
swifter start-ups.

Predator and prey enhance
each other's species, goading
both to hone existing talents,
improvise mutations
benign and beneficial.

But, what about the flies?
What change forthcoming?
No good news for mammals
except to raise the bar.

Christine Irving

When Predator Becomes Prey

It flows like green current through dry grass,
thin forked tongue tasting night's vibration.

Egret perches precariously
on a thin twig barely stout enough
to prove purchase for a toe.
Lacking the antenna
of earthbound animals
she sleeps lightly,
one eye at a time, wary.

Snake sends coils
round the tree trunk,
muscling up with liquid ease.
Down below, a watcher waits,
calculating how close serpent
can slide before bird startles, flies.

Stars move overhead. Creatures mark,
don't measure, time's passing. Don't
track its passage, nor anticipate the next tick.
A talent for patience enhances survival's
chances as often as quick acceleration
from a dead stop, ups odds.

The moment arrives, viper lunges,
egret flaps. They fall. Venom
overpowers wing. Honey badger
barges in for evening's final kill.

he don't care

juggernaut
of fur, claw, reek,
& hungry maw

david to goliath lion
caracal & cheetah

audacious predator
immune to venom
loose-skinned & spry

forever furious
clever, stubborn
omnivorous

honey badger

Christine Irving

Honey Badger Dreaming

Scent slips inside his coma,
enticing as a flash of scale caught
by the corner of a fisherman's eye,

almost enough to shake him
from poisoned slumber
ravenous as any creature
woken from the dead.

But sleep continues,
inertia's dormant strength
compelling obeisance till scent
again insinuates, sliding
musky perfumed nectar
between the layered dreams.

He wakes alert, already
tracking, nose poked high
to catch elusive pheromones—
honeybees! Hive secreted
in high canopy, camouflaged
to no avail amidst the blossoms
of briar-bearing vines.

Also Known as Ratel

Untamed in perpetuity
I go my way—
rough, ungroomed, dusty—
needle tooth and iron claw
forever ready to my service.
I dig, I build, I climb
and burrow. I bite. I scratch.
I tear. I eat and eat, return
from the dead again and again.
Escape is my nature. I give
no warning, no quarter,
my fights always finish.
Alone I live, but not
without community.
No creature like me, none
I would I rather be.

Christine Irving

The Sisterhood

Baby bee, cradled in wax,
dreams of dancing—
already she's addicted.
Sweet honey scent permeates
her nursey, lingers on the breath
of those who tend and feed and groom.

Somewhere, deep inside the hive,
a dancefloor echoes to tapdancing feet
relaying vital vectors.

Soon, she will prance before her sisters,
turning, swaying, sashaying—
lithe as any houri dancing after hours
content with secret perfumed pleasures,
amber nectars laced with attars
of jasmine, gardenia, and musk melon.

Exhaustion, trumping ecstasy,
will collapse her into sleep
while sisters take wing to fly her course.

With luck, no foe will decimate their hive
and they will live their sweet short lives
measured in miles of flight
seeking dusty golden treasure.

Endangered

They die in their thousands.
Tiny furry-winged angels
litter the floors of dead hives,
lie like invisible breadcrumbs
guiding the feet of ghost children
through summer fields
and forests of unrelieved green,
bereft of blueberries, red- cheeked
apples, yellow squash, purple
eggplant, blushing peaches,
the warm brown husks of walnut,
almond, hickory, pecan…

Christine Irving

The Hive in Which We Live

Brazil nuts grow on long-lived hermit trees who stand alone of
all their kind in jungle groves lush with the flora of other clans
and tribes.

> some sentient beings
> choose solitude, the better
> to share their bounty

Only undomesticated orchid bees indigenous to Amazon forests
possess the wherewithal to pick the intricate locked blossoms of
Bertholletia excelsa.

> she unlocks to songs
> known only to the feral–
> winged and wild of heart

The flowers grow in loose branching clusters, each bloom
possessing six cream-colored petals and a multitude of stamens
shaped into a hooded mass.

> sensuality
> unites all species in sweet
> commonality

Fertilized, ripe, the fruit continues practicing its parent's
caution, forming an impenetrable shell. Only three wild
creatures can free the seeds inside.

> nothing thrives alone
> old tales offer help three times
> respect the stranger

The agouti, larger cousin to the guinea pig, gnaws through a soft
spot on the hull especially designed to give way beneath its
sharp incisors.
>   rodent teeth must gnaw
>   lest grown too long they cripple,
>   thoughts need pruning, too

Inside lie eight to twenty-four shell-encased seeds– Brazil nuts–
agouti's treasure chest of fatty food, gorged upon till belly
rounds, remainder cached randomly underground.
>   buried at random
>   forgotten seeds await sunshine
>   to grow gigantic

The beak of the red and green macaw opens Brazil pods with
abandon. Feasting in treetops, abundant fruit in easy reach, they
easily afford the occasional dropped nut.
>   nuts and rusks rain down
>   littering the distant floor
>   nothing wasted here

Pacu, large herbivore fish related to Piranha, possess molar-like
teeth in their lower jaws perfect for crushing the adamantine
rinds of Brazil nut fruits that drop into the river.
>   fruit floats on surface
>   tempting as a flashing lure
>   luscious as a grub

Christine Irving

When Amazon floods, spreading out for acres beneath rainforest
canopy, the fallen fruits float up, pacu extend territories;
boundaries blur, dissolve and disappear, pushing frontiers
forward exponentially.

> floods wipe out fences
> new parameters arise
> life quickens again

Gaia's three-fold distribution system makes commercialization
unfeasible; demand for nuts surpasses supply— slash and burn
diminishes, the need for nut trees halts logging in Brazil.

> she covers her bets
> puts plan B into action
> and then gets cracking

Perhaps we underestimate the long-range backup plans in
place— do not yet see intelligence as Earth's birthright, handed
down across galaxies, inherent in stardust, prime element of this
universe.

> body, mind, and heart
> don't define intelligence
> greater than their sum

On Salmon Creek

Inch by patient inch,
salmon endure.
Moving close,
ever closer
to the cataract
on Salmon Creek.

Silver-scaled fish come fighting,
heeding nature's primal call to breed.
Cells die with every breath,
each twisting leap powered
by muscled flesh still firm,
succulent, sweet.

Bears line the rocky ledge,
dark silhouettes half-hidden
in surging crush of current-driven waters
churned white by eddy, gush and flux,
silky swells ripped to froth and foam
while cubs pace shorelines,
mewling for their mothers.

Fish and bruin feed, spawn, die, thrive
in an ancient pattern of replenishment
dependent on patience, position,
and random notice by trickster gods
taking the shape of ravens
to scavenge for scraps.

Christine Irving

Closing the Circle

Crescent moon cavorts among clouds
silver as a salmon's scale, lithe as fish
that bend and arc, thrusting heavenward
to clear a cataract, sharp silhouettes
leaping across blue days, starlit nights,
redrawn a thousand ways by Haida, Tlingit,
Mi'kmaq, Muckleshoot, and Kwakwaka'wakw.

Moon's sea creatures
subject to tides and currents,
till leaving home, then hurl themselves
upstream curled mouth to tail, struggling
toward source, choosing renewal
for all their relations.

The Cull

Sharp note of undigested resin.
The wounded doe's morning nibble
fails to find the absent elements
expectant body craves.
Limp leaves telegraph a tangled tale—
pain, fear, confusion, pregnancy.

Wolf snuffs twice. Two adolescent cubs
edge up beside him, sniffing eagerly
at pungent snarled scents; distinguishing
specie, gender, emotion; puzzled
by infection and gestation.

Deer flees on ahead. She will turn at the end
to fight for the fawn she carries, sharp hooves
flashing in the sun before blood drains scarlet
into snow, before cub's father gnaws
the gangrened shoulder off bone, dumps it
far from the feast, for ravens to demolish.

Christine Irving

Tracks

The snow tells a bedtime tale
anyone could read.

Rabbitbrush's bare bent branch,
furrows formed by burrowing noses
searching out dry winter grass.

Claws pressed deep in perfect prints
where wolf once lurked, still
as the stone he stood behind.

Stalk.
Chase.
Skirmish.
Escape.
Blood.

Anyone can read snow's story
and say goodnight.

Sometime Between January and March

*During this time, the alpha pair
may move out of the pack
temporarily to prevent interruption
from other pack members.*
~http://www.wolfcountry.net

She wakes restless,
wanting to howl,
but night is black,
stars cloud-shrouded,
pack sleeps soundly,

Almost time.

She sniffs cold air,
detects no hint of spring
and yet paws itch
as if they feel
ground quickening…

Almost time.

Mate's ear twitches.
She nudges, licks, nips.
He wakes alert.
Her scent fills the dark.
He follows
silently
swiftly
into the forest
away from the pack.

Christine Irving

never afterwards the same

Then will the lame leap like a deer,
and the mute tongue shout for joy.
Water will gush forth in the wilderness
and streams in the desert.
~Isaiah 35:6, New International Version

Three deer stand still, fading
in and out amongst dun grasses
slender branches, bare of leaf

frozen in place, I fear to blink
or turn my eye away. They'll disappear,
I know. I cannot bear to see them go.

Deer are not uncommon, these
are not the first nor last I'll see
yet I forbear to startle—

so rapt am I, so tethered.
Delivered into their keeping
by that all-seeing gaze

as if God had opened liquid eyes
to take my full measure.
Terror my bones

irradiates my mind, till I am the deer
looking at me looking back
into raw, primal, terrible, holy love.

What Lasts

I.

A knoll above the sea
becomes stag's final resting.
Unconsigned to bardo or limbo,
his wild soul melds instantly with air.
Flesh and fascia melt quickly.
Fox, badger, skunk scatter bone.
Insects obliterate whatever scraps remain.
Only the antlers survive.

II.

It seems ironic to the boy
that only the transient portion
of the deer's long continuity still lingers.
Lashing rack to backpack he presses on,
leaving the clearing to push through
tangled undergrowth and biting flies
down to the sea.

Dragging lengths of driftwood, he heads
toward far points of tumbled rock.
Arriving, digs a hole, teepees branches
above the deep depression. Covers the limbs
with ground cloth and sleeping bag. Digs again.
Carries stones. Blankets them with tangled sticks
and desiccated seaweed.

Boy swims while fire burns. Salt stings
then sooths each scratch, itch and burn.
Sluices sweat away. He romps naked
in the surf, splashing, leaping, rolling,
tumbling, till embers glow red as setting sun
and he emerges, bathed in reflected glory
like a young god.

Grabbing the antlers, he holds them to his head
dances round the dying fire, screaming defiance,
love, surrender to whichever demons bind him.

Prongs hold glowing rocks, carried carefully
from pit to sipapu. Smoke of burning herbs,
steam of saltwater, carry prayers
requesting the acumen of his ancestors.

III.

Driftwood dispersed, ashes scattered,
antlers abandoned where headland
gives way to water, the boy leaves no trace
to mark his presence. Days later,
or weeks or months, on a distant shore,
a foreign coast, an alien clime,
the antlers reappear, wrapped up in fishline,
laid out on a bed of seagrass
like an offering or a gift.

Wanted

Single mule deer, female,
skilled in self-defense
to care for two newborns.
Must have strong maternal instincts
and sharp ears. Pregnant doe preferred.
Employment temporary, spring
to mid-summer. Whitetail mother
will not be responsible for death
or injury of employee. (Coyote threat
high through week following solstice;
afterwards, threat tapers exponentially.)

Apply at birch grove
north side of pine plantation
near the house without dogs.
Interviews begin at dusk.
Location of morel
mushroom patch
revealed to accepted applicant.

Contact: Whitetail Doe

Christine Irving

Going Naked

Consider the octopus, exiting
shell to wander forever uncovered.
Exposure suited the creature,
sharpened its wit. Clad in slime,
it traveled the edges of seas,
exploring coastal boundaries,
skipping tide pool to tide pool,
feasting on starfish and crab.

Primeval ancestors
prowling sunless depths
needed eyes acute as a woman's,
trading color for dark-adapted vision
till skin reclaimed lost myriad hues,
turning camouflage to art.

Suckers lined the sentient arms—
muscled cups flexible as fingers,
opposable as thumbs, each one
independently manipulated
by an agile active mind.

This cephalopod,
affectionate and ruthless,
more ancient in its lineage
than humankind, knew long ago
what we have yet to learn—
the rampant possibilities
in daring to be naked.

Letter from a Poison Pen

I order the sepia online
from Pittsburg's Premier Pigments.
It takes a fortnight to arrive,
lots of time to think about ink,
how for centuries Romans to Victorians
employed the cephalopod's dark discharge
to fashion letters, expelling words
from here to there across distances
no cry could ever cover. (Even then,
tears splashed upon a page made ugly blots,
obscuring meaning the way a cuttlefish's ink
conceals the fleeing animal.)

I remember how you fled, sending out
false signals deliberately to obfuscate,
plying me with sex and mushrooms,
befuddling my instincts until I lost
all feeling for veracity, failed
to follow logic toward its sad conclusion.

I mix the sepia myself
following a formula of Leonardo,
adding a dose of my own devising.
It smells faintly of the sea
and Bragg's Liquid Aminos,
making me hungry enough to order
risotto al Nero from Pompeii Gardens,
our favorite Friday night go-to.

Those little white lights still twinkle
among purple plastic grapes.
Gino pours chianti with the same
lavish liberal hand. I linger so long
my ink dries and needs remixing.

But now it's finished.
I burn the residue,
lick the envelope,
seal it with a kiss of death.

Farewell my dear chameleon,
addio.

The Shedding

Molting soft shell dove deep.
Naked, sought the dark
wondering what she'd shed
and why?
Regrets and wild yearning
burbled behind her crying,
"Look back,"
look back…"

Still she swam,
thrashing naked arms
through strange waters.

By degrees,
the tides claimed her;
Earth's heartbeat
pushed awkward arms
into new rhythms.
Round and red they grew;
carapace hardened,
turned blue

Until one night she rose,
bedecked in queenly color,
swimming up moonbeams
to find her place among the stars.

Christine Irving

The Crab Goddess Guides Her Daughter

Yemanjá, Queen of the Ocean,
patron spirit to fishermen
and survivors of shipwrecks,
is feminine principle of creation,
and the spirit of moonlight.
~Wikipedia: Yemoja (paraphrased)

She scuttles sidewise,
heading for the sea.
Yemanjá's slender silver claw,
glows bright on the horizon
guiding her through bracken,
over fallen fronds of palm.

She has waited, waited,
storing sperm,
desperately searching
any source of water
to dampen gills, breathe
and keep breathing.

When moon signal appears,
gravid, ready to lay her
hundred thousand eggs
in Yemanjá's salt waters,
she scuttles sidewise
heading for the sea.

On Hearing of His Sister's Death

The news of his sister's death
took five months to reach him, traveling
through resident pods at speed—
in clicks, trills and a staticky buzz
perfected by the matriarchs—
a genealogical shorthand
used by daughters, aunts, cousins
for gossip and daily updates of mating,
pregnancy, demise and schooling fishes.
More laconic transient orcas, leaner, meaner,
keep themselves to themselves, hunting
in tight packs of three or four.

He'd swum with his mother and sisters
a few years, but somehow the females
sensed each other more readily, in elusive
ways more visceral, fluid, and swift
than he could master. It weighed on him
and he grew restless. One day, lagging
to flag an elusive seal, he lost them, learned
to forage by himself, making pals here
and there, hooking up intermittently,
often content with solitude.

Christine Irving

The dirge reached his ears near an atoll
in Caribbean waters. The lament held riffs
from his sister's signature song. It held
his mother's grief, the loneliness of two
where three once roamed together.
Swimming north he reshaped the requiem,
reciting the roll of their grandmothers,
the thrill of hunting in packs, adding
an intimation of return.

To Hunt

Orcas run deep,
silent as submarines
or racket around
half-submerged,
fins above the waterline,
hunting in packs,
herding, stalking,
moving together
to kill.

Christine Irving

Zoochosis

Animals go mad in zoos.
Crazed by confinement
and boredom, she paces.
He swims figure-eights
all day and night. Finally,
worn to exhaustion,
sweet sleep takes them home
to acre upon acre of lush
green lands, pack, and prey;
to fierce, fine fishing and sleepy
harems of sleek plump flesh
sprawled on a pebbled beach.

In Hope of a Hundredth Seal

Undersea lies
a sunken horizon
beyond which light fails
to penetrate the deep.
Great Whites prowl here.

In this dim twilit zone
where sight still acts as sense
but dusk dims vision, a seal pup,
intent on calculations
of turn and counterturn,
pursues his own swift chase.

Hidden in the dark below
mother watches, waits. Stiff
vibrissae whiskers track the shark's
position, note every subtle surge
of muscle, signal when to move.

Sleek as a torpedo, she shoots
toward predator. Spinning,
gathering momentum, slams herself
against fish using the rebound
to jackknife away.

Christine Irving

She learned this trick watching dolphins—
Shark's blood-rich liver lies right beneath its skin.
Hard head butt, in the perfect spot, explodes it.

If they survive the Great White, the seal
will pass the dolphins' tactic onto pups.
With luck her lesson will spread, animal
to animal in other far-flung colonies.

Be Wary of Wishing

Prey, he thinks, should be worthy
of a man, bigger than a man, stronger,
more muscled. He flexes biceps,
thumps abs, ready to test himself
against the wild. Never having known
necessity, he calls himself predator.

Prey, she thinks, must be small, helpless,
outmuscled, victimized. She fantasizes
alphas taking her by force, devours pulp fiction
featuring vampires and werewolves.
In nightmares, she is always being chased.

They have yet to walk into a dark wood
alone on a moonless night where Nature
needs no creature, aids or spite to test
one's mettle. Forests make noises, the way
sleeping mammals grunt, snort, fart,
twitch and turn through dreams. Tree limbs
bump and scrape, twigs snap. Pinecones
fall to ground, leaves whisper, each sound
magnified by surrounding silence as if
some frightened wanderer, intrusive and naïve,
caught unaware, holds breath and trembles.

They have yet to meet the Other
who paints her fingernails scarlet,
chews betel nuts that redden teeth.
The one who stirs her cauldron of chaos
and lo— domestic pigs turn feral, saber-
toothed honey badgers hunt cobras.

Christine Irving

The Danger of Uninformed Assumption

Malarial mosquitos who once lived happily in rainforest canopies content to dine on arboreal creatures, move to ground when forests are cut. Whereafter, rates of infected humans rise dramatically.

> mother mosquitos
> craving but a drop of blood
> pursue human prey

We were taught the food chain arranges itself in straightforward hierarchies, moving down in stepped pyramids from those bigger/stronger/fiercer to the smaller/weaker/softer.

> might makes right— a creed
> backed up by wise men's science—
> refuted by bugs

A Quartet of Considerations

I. Where Buffalo Once Roamed

Will's wife calls him a "peach of a guy,"
but he strings dead coyotes along the fence.
Maybe he forgot the yellow school bus
stops by their front gate each day. Didn't
think the putrid miasma, worse than skunk,
would cling like red dust to the curls of girls
and collars of boys who wait in the sun
beside the dry canal that forms a practical
depository for sun-bleached bone and hide.
Doesn't understand why frightened daughter
shies away, why truculent son transfers
that elusive gaze to some distant point
beyond his father's left shoulder.

II. To Trust a Trickster

The moon, juicy as a ripe peach,
drips amber light into the dry canal.
Fifty quiet men slip from a rickety bus,
follow their coyote's footprints
through fine dust to river's bank.
Fence stretches like a choke collar
across the frightening frontier. They smell
skunk, riverweed, dust and tobacco.
Up ahead by a dark gate, lights blink
three times three signaling safe transfer
to another life. Suddenly, it becomes
practical to pray, imperative to believe.

III. Too Little, Too Late

This mahogany forest
desperately needs a doctor.
Purple spots bruise every leaf,
oozing contagious slime.
The insidious infection spreads
through air, water, human contact.
Even cameras disperse disease,
drone images lethal as live spores.
The trees will soon exist only in memoir,
nubs of old trunks sold as earrings
at auctions held to galvanize a public
unwilling, unready, ridiculously unafraid…

IV. A Lie Repeated Thrice

The prosecutor stormed and raged,
framed his argument in bombast,
and flying accusations until, triggered
by flamboyant rhetoric, outrage
filled every inch of courtroom space.
Defense attorney barked. Judge
pounded gavel. "Going swimmingly,"
the lawyer thought, renewing the attack,
never adding up his soul's cost
in disregarded oaths, vows he'd made
but never meant to keep.
Afterward the press came running,
recording, yet again. how easily
the threefold lie will vanquish truth.

The Ornithologist Speaks Her Mind

*Military researchers in the US develop
a new breed of unmanned drones
... the size of birds and even bugs.*
~The Telegraph, Oct. 07, 2015

You inquire about
the kingfisher's feathers—
their exact shade of blue,
the number of pinions,
the chemical composition
of oil produced in the gland
beneath each wing,
taken by beak
to coat quill and vane—
a light oil,
like the viscous fluid
found floating in hollow chambers
of sperm whale skulls, more precious
than gold dissolved in sea water.

Our seas hold secrets yet more dear—
the sandpaper durability of sharkskin,
or the tiny bumps on the tail of humpbacks.

Science the Seductress mimics
nature's secrets, tempts the curious
to demystify the miraculous,
transmogrify complex adaptations
into tricky soldiers' toys, saving bodies,
but shattering minds whose only salvation
lies in the mysterious alchemy
between bare fingers and toes
thrust into ordinary dirt, the sweet
exhilaration of swinging birches,
or the rapt contemplation
of a kingfisher's feathers.

> First line from Pablo
> Neruda's *Enigmas*
> ~ trans. by Robert Bly

Christine Irving

About the Author

Christine Irving is the author of several volumes of poetry, two novels, one hybrid and a smatter of other works. She is a passionate advocate of the spoken word and loves to read and perform her poetry aloud.

Christine learned long ago to "walk her poems" – voicing them as she paces in order to feel and hear the rhythm of the words. It is the relationship between craft and content, left and right brain that most fascinates her about creativity, thus her work focuses on revealing the myriad connections which hold the world together.

As always in her work, the poetry in this volume incorporates a life-long study of Jungian psychology and world myth. The animal world figures predominantly in symbology and reflects humankind's long intimate relationship with the rest of the natural world. That this relationship has in recent centuries been sadly truncated and erodes more quickly every day is a source of constant grief. The desire to honor her fellow animals and bring them to greater consciousness prompted the writing of *Predator/Prey*.

To discover more about her work or to contact Christine, visit her website at:
http://www.christineirving.com/

or follow her blog
https://magdalenesmuse.wordpress.com/

68

Christine Irving

Also by Christine Irving

Poetry

Be a Teller of Tales
The Naked Man
You Can Tell a Crone By Her Cackle
Sitting on the Hag Seat: A Celtic Knot of Poems
Return to Inanna
Ping Pong Poetry (with Susan Maxwell Campbell)
Poetic License

Hybrid

Sun Strokes: An Illuminated Pastiche
    of Collage, Poetry & Prose

Novels

Magdalene A.D.
The Mystery of the Black Madonna (Juvenile)

Travel

Motorcycle Dreaming: Riding the 'Beauty Way'
    Back in Time Across America

Almanac

Celtic Wheel of the Year

Script

A Rose in Winter (with Kathryn Smith)